SACRED SPACE

for Lent 2015

from the website www.sacredspace.ie
Prayer from the Irish Jesuits

ave maria press AᴹA notre dame, indiana

Acknowledgment

The publisher would like to thank Piaras Jackson, S.J., and Alan McGuckian, S.J., for their kind assistance in making this book possible. Correspondence with the Sacred Space team can be directed to feedback@sacredspace.ie where comments or suggestions related to the book or to www.sacredspace.ie will always be welcome.

Unless otherwise noted, the Scripture quotations contained herein are from the *New Revised Standard Version* of the Bible, copyright © 1989 by the Division of Christian Education of the National Council of the Churches of Christ in the United States of America. Used by permission. All rights reserved.

Published under license from Michelle Anderson Publishing Pty Ltd., in Australia.

Founded in 1865, Ave Maria Press is a ministry of the Indiana Province of Holy Cross.

www.avemariapress.com

Paperback: ISBN-13 978-1-59471-554-9

E-book: ISBN-13 978-1-59471-555-6

Cover design by Andy Wagoner.

Text design by Kristen Hornyak Bonelli.

Printed and bound in the United States of America.

SACRED
SPACE

for Lent 2015

"The website *Sacred Space* has been helping millions to pray for some years. Now Ave Maria Press makes these very helpful and easily usable prayer-helps available in handsome and accessible form, including pocket-sized booklets for the Advent/Christmas and Lenten seasons. What a great service to God's people! I hope millions more will buy the books. God is being well served."

William A. Barry, S.J.
Author of *Paying Attention to God*

How to Use This Book

During this Lenten season, we invite you to make a sacred space in your day. Spend ten minutes praying here and now, wherever you are, with the help of a prayer guide and scripture chosen specially for each day. Every place is a sacred space, so you may wish to have this little book available at any time or place during the course of the day: in your desk at work, while traveling, on your bedside table, in your purse or jacket pocket. . . . Remember that God is everywhere, all around us, constantly reaching out to us, even in the most unlikely situations. When we know this, and with a bit of practice, we can pray anywhere.

The following pages will guide you through a session of prayer stages.

Something to think and pray about each
    day this week
The Presence of God
Freedom
Consciousness
The Word (leads you to the daily Lenten
    scripture and provides help with the
    text)
Conversation
Conclusion

It is most important to come back to these
pages each day of the week, as they are an integral part of each day's prayer and lead to the
scripture and inspiration points.

Although written in the first person, the
prayers are for "doing" rather than for reading
out. Each stage is a kind of exercise or meditation aimed at helping you to get in touch with
God and God's presence in your life.

We hope that you will join the many people around the world praying with us in our sacred space.

The Presence of God

Bless all who worship you, almighty
God,
from the rising of the sun to its setting:
from your goodness enrich us,
by your love inspire us,
by your Spirit guide us,
by your power protect us,
in your mercy receive us,
now and always.

February 18—21

Something to think and pray about each day this week:

Exploring Our Space

In our cities the social supports for the sabbath have disappeared. In commercial and social terms, a Sunday is barely different from a weekday. There can be a blessing in this change. Jesus constantly shifted the emphasis from law to love, and we can learn to do the same. We can learn to think of the sabbath as a time to find space for God rather than focus on the guilt of missing Mass or doing a job. Generations of parents have worried themselves sick over their children ignoring church laws, not unlike the rabbis in Jesus' time.

It might be more productive to focus first on making Sunday special in some way, and then on making space for God. Many German households still make the family meal on Sunday the highest priority of the week, more important than any sport or other distraction. Dublin, the seedbed of *Sacred Space*, sees a great population of ramblers take to the hills on Sunday: the pleasures of the hike, and the change of tempo from work or study, are balm to the soul as well as the body. We get in touch with God in different ways, through sitting with our family over a meal, through taking time out to stop and stare at God's creation, through joining the community of our neighbors in the ancient but simple shared worship of the Mass.

The Presence of God

At any time of the day or night
we can call on Jesus.
He is always waiting,
listening for our call.
What a wonderful blessing!
No phone needed, no e-mails,
just a whisper.

Freedom

I will ask God's help,
to be free from my own preoccupations,
to be open to God in this time of prayer,
to come to love and serve him more.

Consciousness

How am I really feeling? Light-hearted?
Heavy-hearted?
I may be very much at peace, happy to be
here.
Equally, I may be frustrated, worried, or angry.

I acknowledge how I really am.
It is the real me that the Lord loves.

The Word

The Word of God comes down to us through
the scriptures. May the Holy Spirit enlighten
my mind and my heart to respond to the
gospel teachings. (Each day turn to the cor-
responding scripture on the following pages.
Inspiration points are there should you need
them. When you are ready, return here to
continue.)

Conversation

Remembering that I am
still in God's presence,
I imagine Jesus himself sitting beside me,
and I say whatever is on my mind,
whatever is in my heart,
speaking as one friend to another.

Conclusion

Glory be to the Father, and to the Son, and to the Holy Spirit,

As it was in the beginning, is now, and ever shall be,

world without end. Amen.

Wednesday 18th February, Ash Wednesday
Matthew 6:1—6

Beware of practicing your piety before others in order to be seen by them; for then you have no reward from your Father in heaven. So whenever you give alms, do not sound a trumpet before you, as the hypocrites do in the synagogues and in the streets, so that they may be praised by others. Truly I tell you, they have received their reward. But when you give alms, do not let your left hand know what your right hand is doing, so that your alms may be done in secret; and your Father who sees in secret will reward you. And whenever you pray, do not be like the hypocrites; for they love to stand and pray in the synagogues and at the street corners, so that they may be seen by others. Truly I tell you, they have received their reward. But whenever you pray, go to your room and shut the door and pray to your Father who is in secret; and your Father who sees in secret will reward you."

- Lent is a time to recall the priority of God in our lives: that we come from and go to God, and that God is the companion of our lives. The focus of living faith and religious practice is not on us, but on God's place in our lives.

- Ash Wednesday 2015 means nine years of the *Sacred Space for Lent* books. It may be good, in prayer, to think of the others who will pray with this book today. We are not alone as we pray.

Thursday 19th February
Luke 9:22—25

Jesus said to his disciples: "The Son of Man must suffer greatly and be rejected by the elders, chief priests, and scribes, and be killed, and on the third day be raised." Then he said to them all, "If any want to become my followers, let them deny themselves and take up their cross daily and follow me. For those who want to save their life will lose it, and those who lose their life for my sake will save it. What does it profit them if they gain the whole world, but lose or forfeit themselves?"

- The big mystery of Lent is the death and resurrection of the Lord.

- As he carried a cross, we too carry crosses throughout our lives in the difficulties and weaknesses of body, mind, and spirit. We save our lives in giving ourselves away in love to God and to others.

Friday 20th February
Matthew 9:14—15

Then the disciples of John came to Jesus, saying, "Why do we and the Pharisees fast often, but your disciples do not fast?" And Jesus said to them, "The wedding guests cannot mourn as long as the bridegroom is with them, can they? The days will come when the bridegroom is taken away from them, and then they will fast."

- No matter what mystery of Jesus' life we go to in prayer, we can rejoice. Even in his suffering and death, he is with us, and we do not mourn. Without his presence in our lives, we would truly mourn the loss of something and someone really relevant and essential to our lives.

- Today, let me focus on the place of Jesus in my life.

Saturday 21st February
Luke 5:27—32

After this Jesus went out and saw a tax collector named Levi sitting at the tax booth, and he said to him, "Follow me." And he got up, left everything, and followed him. Then Levi gave a great banquet for him in his house, and there was a large crowd of tax collectors and others sitting at the table with them. The Pharisees and their scribes were complaining to his disciples, saying, "Why do you eat and drink with tax collectors and sinners?" Jesus answered, "Those who are well have no need of a physician, but those who are sick; I have come to call not the righteous but sinners to repentance."

- Jesus mixed with the riff-raff, with people who were outcasts in the society of the time. We see the same when he speaks with and heals people with leprosy. His eye seems to find the person who most needs the look of love and the power of his healing.

- The eye of Jesus will look with love on that part of each of us which needs the power of his healing love. He surprises us.

February 22—February 28

Something to think and pray about each day this week:

A Lenten Resolution

As we move into Lent, we might be wondering if fasting has any meaning for us today. It does. It is really asking us to look at our relationship to food and drink. Jesus loved to eat with his friends. Meals were important for him. For families too, meals are a time when children watch and listen to their parents and vice versa. But family meals are in danger of disappearing—what with fast food, the lure of electronic games, and TV that is sometimes left on even when the family is eating together. Like talking on the phone in company, it reduces our presence to one another. For many families a good Lenten resolution would be to have meals together at least once a week and expose themselves to the need for listening, sitting at peace, knowing how the rest of the family is, and going for slow rather than fast food.

The Presence of God

Jesus waits silent and unseen to come into my heart.
I will respond to his call.
He comes with his infinite power and love.
May I be filled with joy in his presence.

Freedom

I ask for the grace
to let go of my own concerns
and be open to what God is asking of me,
to let myself be guided and formed by my loving Creator.

Consciousness

Knowing that God loves me unconditionally,
I can afford to be honest about how I am.

How has the last day been, and how do I feel now?

I share my feelings openly with the Lord.

The Word

I read the Word of God slowly, a few times over, and I listen to what God is saying to me. (Please turn to your scripture on the following pages. Inspiration points are there should you need them. When you are ready, return here to continue.)

Conversation

Remembering that I am still in God's presence, I imagine Jesus himself standing or sitting beside me,

and say whatever is on my mind, whatever is in my heart,

speaking as one friend to another.

Conclusion

Glory be to the Father, and to the Son, and to the Holy Spirit,

As it was in the beginning, is now, and ever shall be,

World without end. Amen.

Sunday 22nd February,
First Sunday of Lent
Mark 1:12—15

And the Spirit immediately drove him out into the wilderness. He was in the wilderness forty days, tempted by Satan; and he was with the wild beasts; and the angels waited on him. Now after John was arrested, Jesus came to Galilee, proclaiming the good news of God, and saying, "The time is fulfilled, and the kingdom of God has come near; repent, and believe in the good news."

- I, too, have known times of temptation when I felt on my own except for the wild beasts, the irrational forces that were messing up my life.

- Lord, you felt the influence of evil and were tested. You were purified as you came through a difficult time. When I was in the middle of such a time, it did not feel like God's hand, but like desolation and despair. When I look back, I can see how God was shaping me.

Monday 23rd February
Matthew 25:31—40

When the Son of Man comes in his glory, and all the angels with him, then he will sit on the throne of his glory. All the nations will be gathered before him, and he will separate people one from another as a shepherd separates the sheep from the goats, and he will put the sheep at his right hand and the goats at the left. Then the king will say to those at his right hand, 'Come, you that are blessed by my Father, inherit the kingdom prepared for you from the foundation of the world; for I was hungry and you gave me food, I was thirsty and you gave me something to drink, I was a stranger and you welcomed me, I was naked and you gave me clothing, I was sick and you took care of me, I was in prison and you visited me.' Then the righteous will answer him, 'Lord, when was it that we saw you hungry and gave you food, or thirsty and gave you something to drink? And when was it that we saw you a stranger and welcomed you, or naked and gave you clothing? And when was it that we saw you sick or in prison and visited you?' And the king will answer them, 'Truly I tell you, just as you did it to one of the least of these who are members of my family, you did it to me.'"

- How and where do I find God? These questions are often raised today and were raised with Jesus too. He gives many answers, but a strong answer is that in the poorest of the poor, we find Jesus. What we do for them, we do for him.

- Does this parable surprise me? Do I "get it" yet? Can I pray about needy people I know and see in them the light and the need of Jesus Christ?

Tuesday 24th February
Matthew 6:7–15

Jesus said, "When you are praying, do not heap up empty phrases as the Gentiles do; for they think that they will be heard because of their many words. Do not be like them, for your Father knows what you need before you ask him. Pray then in this way: 'Our Father in heaven, hallowed be your name. Your kingdom come. Your will be done, on earth as it is in heaven. Give us this day our daily bread. And forgive us our debts, as we also have forgiven our debtors. And do not bring us to the time of trial, but rescue us from the evil one.' For if you forgive others their trespasses, your heavenly Father will also forgive you; but if you do not forgive others, neither will your Father forgive your trespasses."

- Prayer engages us in praise of God, in desiring God's will to be done and God's kingdom to come on earth; in prayer we ask for what we

need for the day, and for the grace of forgiveness
for self and others, and to stay on the path of our
love and convictions.

• Lord, teach me to pray like this each day.

Wednesday 25th February
Luke 11:29—32

When the crowds were increasing, [Jesus]
began to say, "This generation is an evil
generation; it asks for a sign, but no sign will be
given to it except the sign of Jonah. For just as
Jonah became a sign to the people of Nineveh,
so the Son of Man will be to this generation.
The queen of the South will rise at the judgment with the people of this generation and condemn them, because she came from the ends of
the earth to listen to the wisdom of Solomon,
and see, something greater than Solomon is
here! The people of Nineveh will rise up at the
judgment with this generation and condemn it,
because they repented at the proclamation of

Jonah, and see, something greater than Jonah is here!"

- Jonah was a man of narrow religious beliefs and intolerant of God's gracious treatment of Nineveh's pagan people. Yet the people believed in God and ultimately did God's will.

- Jesus is saying to us that the people of this pagan city had greater faith than the people to whom he spoke. He asks us for at least as much wisdom in hearing his word as the people of Nineveh had in hearing Jonah.

Thursday 26th February
Matthew 7:7—12

Ask, and it will be given you; search, and you will find; knock, and the door will be opened for you. For everyone who asks receives, and everyone who searches finds, and for everyone who knocks, the door will be opened. Is there anyone among you who, if your child asks for bread, will give a stone? Or if the child asks for a fish, will give a snake? If you then, who are evil, know how to give good gifts to your children, how much more will your Father in heaven give good things to those who ask him!

"In everything do to others as you would have them do to you; for this is the law and the prophets."

- In the asking is the receiving, in the searching is the finding, in the knocking is the opening. No prayer is wasted. All prayer, like all love, bears its own fruit in its own season.

- Lord, teach me to know that you are always listening, and to accept that being heard is good enough in itself.

Friday 27th February
Matthew 5:20–24

Jesus said to his disciples, "For I tell you, unless your righteousness exceeds that of the scribes and Pharisees, you will never enter the kingdom of heaven. You have heard that it was said to those of ancient times, 'You shall not murder'; and 'Whoever murders shall be liable to judgment.' But I say to you that if you are angry with a brother or sister, you will be liable to judgment; and if you insult a brother or sister, you will be liable to the council; and if you say, 'You fool,' you will be liable to the hell of fire. So when you are offering your gift at the altar, if you remember that your brother or sister has something against you, leave your gift there before the altar and go; first be reconciled to your brother or sister, and then come and offer your gift."

- We can get stuck in our prayer, dwelling on those who have hurt us: the abusers, the unjust, those we struggle to forgive.

- Jesus knows this. The effect in prayer can be to allow grace to flow into the past, and know that God in Jesus is accompanying us in our hurt.

We may ask the grace to forgive sometime, if not now.

Saturday 28th February
Matthew 5:43—48

J esus said to the disciples, "You have heard that it was said, 'You shall love your neighbor and hate your enemy.' But I say to you, Love your enemies and pray for those who persecute you, so that you may be children of your Father in heaven; for he makes his sun rise on the evil and on the good, and sends rain on the righteous and on the unrighteous. For if you love those who love you, what reward do you have? Do not even the tax collectors do the same? And if you greet only your brothers and sisters, what more are you doing than others? Do not even the Gentiles do the same? Be perfect, therefore, as your heavenly Father is perfect."

• Jesus' sobering words about enemies come into our prayer again today. The bar is set high—love even your enemies. At other times Jesus is more gentle.

- We need to put both sides together—the comforting and the challenging. Maybe he is content with our desire to forgive, and understands with compassion when we cannot.

- We can always pray for the enemy, for the one who has done us harm. This is the beginning, and may one day be forgiveness.

March 1-7

Something to think and pray about each day this week:

A Fast for Today

Fasting has changed because food has changed. In the Western world it is rare for anyone to die of starvation, though plenty of people suffer from malnutrition—through eating too much fat, sugar, or salt. Food has changed its meaning from being just an essential for survival to being a source of pleasure, temptation, and bargaining between children and their parents. In our culture, weight and eating habits are a highly charged topic, to be approached with sensitivity. But for each of us, Lent can offer energy and opportunity to move towards a happier use of food and drink. It is only when we try to

change our habits that we discover how free or
how shackled we are.

The Presence of God

For a few moments, I think of God's veiled
presence in things:
in the elements, giving them existence;
in plants, giving them life;
in animals, giving them sensation;
and finally, in me, giving me all this and more,
making me a temple, a dwelling-place of the
Spirit.

Freedom

God is not foreign to my freedom.
Instead the Spirit breathes life into my most
intimate desires,
gently nudging me towards all that is good.
I ask for the grace to let myself be enfolded by
the Spirit.

Consciousness

Knowing that God loves me unconditionally,
I can afford to be honest about how I am.
How has the last day been, and how do I feel
now?
I share my feelings openly with the Lord.

The Word

The Word of God comes down to us through
the scriptures. May the Holy Spirit enlighten
my mind and my heart to respond to the
gospel teachings. (Please turn to your scripture
on the following pages. Inspiration points are
there should you need them. When you are
ready, return here to continue.)

Conversation

How has God's Word moved me? Has it left
me cold?
Has it consoled me or moved me to act in a
new way?

I imagine Jesus standing or sitting beside me,
I turn and share my feelings with him.

Conclusion

Glory be to the Father, and to the Son, and to
the Holy Spirit,
As it was in the beginning, is now, and ever
shall be,
World without end. Amen.

Sunday 1st March,
Second Sunday of Lent
Mark 9:2—10

Six days later, Jesus took with him Peter and James and John, and led them up a high mountain apart, by themselves. And he was transfigured before them, and his clothes became dazzling white, such as no one on earth could bleach them. And there appeared to them Elijah with Moses, who were talking with Jesus. Then Peter said to Jesus, "Rabbi, it is good for us to be here; let us make three dwellings, one for you, one for Moses, and one for Elijah." He did not know what to say, for they were terrified. Then a cloud overshadowed them, and from the cloud there came a voice, "This is my Son, the Beloved; listen to him!" Suddenly when they looked around, they saw no one with them any more, but only Jesus. As they were coming down the mountain, he ordered them to tell no one about what they had seen, until after the Son of Man had risen from the dead. So they kept the matter to themselves, questioning what this rising from the dead could mean.

- In our journey to God we have peak moments, when the ground is holy. Like Peter, we want them to last forever.

- But Jesus, "only Jesus," brings us down the mountain and prepares us for the hard times ahead, sustained by the memory of brief transfigurations.

- Can I recall any of my peak moments?

Monday 2nd March
Luke 6:36—38

Jesus said to his disciples, "Be merciful, just as your Father is merciful. Do not judge, and you will not be judged; do not condemn, and you will not be condemned. Forgive, and you will be forgiven; give, and it will be given to you. A good measure, pressed down, shaken together, running over, will be put into your lap; for the measure you give will be the measure you get back."

- A generous heart and mind is an immense reward that comes from God. Even in human terms we are enhanced by our qualities of mercy, forgiveness, and tolerance.

- Let us allow prayer to give us the energy of love to burn away some of the bitterness and grudges that are part of every life.

Tuesday 3rd March
Matthew 23:1–12

Then Jesus said to the crowds and to his disciples, "The scribes and the Pharisees sit on Moses' seat; therefore, do whatever they teach you and follow it; but do not do as they do, for they do not practice what they teach. They tie up heavy burdens, hard to bear, and lay them on the shoulders of others; but they themselves are unwilling to lift a finger to move them. They do all their deeds to be seen by others; for they make their phylacteries broad and their fringes long. They love to have the place of honour at banquets and the best seats in the synagogues, and to be greeted with respect in the marketplaces, and to have people call them rabbi. But you are not to be called rabbi, for you have one teacher, and you are all students. And call no one your father on earth, for you have one Father—the one in heaven. Nor are you to be called instructors, for you have one instructor, the Messiah. The greatest among you will be your servant. All who exalt themselves will be humbled, and all who humble themselves will be exalted."

- We can easily think of people who are puffed up with their own praise and a sort of pomposity about themselves. We don't like that in others; there may be a bit in each of us.

- To realize that we are totally dependent on God for life and love is a humbling realization. Prayer at its best keeps us humble, calmed by the warmth of God's love.

Wednesday 4th March
Matthew 20:20–28

Then the mother of the sons of Zebedee came to him with her sons, and kneeling before him, she asked a favor of him. And he said to her, "What do you want?" She said to him, "Declare that these two sons of mine will sit, one at your right hand and one at your left, in your kingdom." But Jesus answered, "You do not know what you are asking. Are you able to drink the cup that I am about to drink?" They said to him, "We are able." He said to them, "You will indeed drink my cup, but to sit at my right hand and at my left, this is not mine to grant, but it is for those for whom it has been prepared by my Father." When the ten heard it, they were angry with the two brothers. But Jesus called them to him and said, "You know that the rulers of the Gentiles lord it over them, and their great ones are tyrants over them. It will not be so among you; but whoever wishes to be great among you must be your servant, and whoever wishes to be first among you must be your slave; just as the Son of Man came not to be served but to serve, and to give his life a ransom for many."

- Greatness with Jesus has little to do with success; it has to do with being like a slave, at the service of master or mistress.

- But a slave in those times also was an honored member of the family. We are glad to be slaves in this sense—the ones who live for the service of God and are honored by God in love.

Thursday 5th March
Luke 16:19—31

Jesus said to the Pharisees, "There was a rich man who was dressed in purple and fine linen and who feasted sumptuously every day. And at his gate lay a poor man named Lazarus, covered with sores, who longed to satisfy his hunger with what fell from the rich man's table; even the dogs would come and lick his sores. The poor man died and was carried away by the angels to be with Abraham. The rich man also died and was buried. In Hades, where he was being tormented, he looked up and saw Abraham far away with Lazarus by his side. He called out, 'Father Abraham, have mercy on me, and send Lazarus to dip the tip of his finger in water and cool my tongue; for I am in agony in these flames.' But Abraham said, 'Child, remember that during your lifetime you received your good things, and Lazarus in like manner evil things; but now he is comforted here, and you are in agony. Besides all this, between you and us a great chasm has been fixed, so that those who might want to pass from here to you cannot do so, and no one can cross from there to us.' He said, 'Then, father, I beg you to send him to my father's house—for I have five brothers—that he may warn them, so that they will not also come into this place of torment.' Abraham replied, 'They have Moses and the prophets; they should listen to them.' He said, 'No, father Abraham; but if someone goes to them from the dead, they will repent.' He said to him, 'If they do not listen to Moses and the prophets, neither will they be convinced even if someone rises from the dead.'"

- This story reminds us of the huge inequality of people in Jesus' time and still today. The parable invites us to see ourselves as richer in the goods of the world than many millions.

- This story challenges us to care for the needy in whatever way we can. Do I accept the challenge?

Friday 6th March
Matthew 21:33—43

Listen to another parable. There was a landowner who planted a vineyard, put a fence around it, dug a wine press in it, and built a watchtower. Then he leased it to tenants and went to another country. When the harvest time had come, he sent his slaves to the tenants to collect his produce. But the tenants seized his slaves and beat one, killed another, and stoned another. Again he sent other slaves, more than the first; and they treated them in the same way. Finally he sent his son to them, saying, "They will respect my son.' But when the tenants saw the son, they said to themselves, "This is the heir; come, let us kill him and get his inheritance.' So they seized him, threw him out of the vineyard, and killed him. Now when the owner of the vineyard comes, what will he do to those tenants?" They said to him, "He will put those wretches to a miserable death, and lease the vineyard to other tenants who will give him the produce at the harvest time." Jesus said to them, "Have you never read in the scriptures: 'The stone that the builders rejected has become the cornerstone; this was the Lord's doing, and it is amazing in our eyes'? Therefore I tell you, the kingdom of God will be taken away from you and given to a people that produces the fruits of the kingdom."

- The stone at the top of the arch holds the arch together. Without its strength and correct positioning, the arch falls. Jesus is the rejected one who has become the centre of our faith and our lives.

- When Jesus is rejected, it only strengthens his relationship with his father, who makes him the keystone and the centre of gospel-faith. He knows our weakness and the pain of rejection; is this what makes us want to be close to him and to follow him closely?

Saturday 7th March
Luke 15:22—24

But the father said to his slaves, "Quickly, bring out a robe—the best one—and put it on him; put a ring on his finger and sandals on his feet. And get the fatted calf and kill it, and let us eat and celebrate; for this son of mine was dead and is alive again; he was lost and is found!"

- We probably know the Prodigal Son story well. It has been called the best short story ever written. It is more about the love of the father than about the sin of the son. It is about the celebration of a loved one's return to God and love.

- Nowhere is the son called to repentance or conversion—it's as if this will happen in the atmosphere of love and forgiveness.

- How can I respond in my life, today?

March 8—14

Something to think and pray about each day this week:

Best Practice

There was a time when Church laws about fasting spelled out in detail the size and weight of what was allowed at main meals or snacks (collations as they were called). In our culture that makes no sense. Fasting, for us, means aiming to keep our personal freedom in face of ingrained habits, which may be habits of eating too much or too little or of eating the wrong sort of food or drink. There is still room for resolutions, but remember: a resolution becomes real not when we make it or write it down, but when we first put it into practice.

The Presence of God

What is present to me is what has a hold on
my becoming.
I reflect on the presence of God always there in
love,
amidst the many things that have a hold on
me.
I pause and pray that I may let God
affect my becoming in this precise moment.

Freedom

There are very few people
who realize what God would make of them
if they abandoned themselves into his hands,
and let themselves be formed by his grace. (St.
Ignatius)
I ask for the grace to trust myself totally to
God's love.

Consciousness

In the presence of my loving Creator,

I look honestly at my feelings over the last day:
the highs, the lows, and the level ground.
Can I see where the Lord has been present?

The Word

God speaks to each one of us individually. I
need to listen to hear what he is saying to me.
Read the text a few times, then listen. (Please
turn to your scripture on the following pages.
Inspiration points are there should you need
them. When you are ready, return here to
continue.)

Conversation

What is stirring in me as I pray?
Am I consoled, troubled, left cold?
I imagine Jesus himself standing or sitting at
my side,
and share my feelings with him.

Conclusion

Glory be to the Father, and to the Son, and to the Holy Spirit,

As it was in the beginning, is now, and ever shall be,

World without end. Amen.

Sunday 8th March,
Third Sunday of Lent
John 2:13—17

The Passover of the Jews was near, and Jesus went up to Jerusalem. In the temple he found people selling cattle, sheep, and doves, and the money changers seated at their tables. Making a whip of cords, he drove all of them out of the temple, both the sheep and the cattle. He also poured out the coins of the money changers and overturned their tables. He told those who were selling the doves, "Take these things out of here! Stop making my Father's house a marketplace!" His disciples remembered that it was written, "Zeal for your house will consume me."

- What was it that roused Jesus' fury? Not just that money changed hands and animals were sold for sacrifice in the Temple; but the fact that the merchants were selling animals at a far higher price in the Temple than would be paid outside and changing money at a rate that brought undue profit to the money changers.

- The hucksters and money changers were profiteering from people's piety, exercising a kind of monopoly that battened on the goodwill of the worshippers. Trade had taken over from prayer.

Monday 9th March
Luke 4:24—30

Jesus said, "Truly I tell you, no prophet is accepted in the prophet's hometown. But the truth is, there were many widows in Israel in the time of Elijah, when the heaven was shut up three years and six months, and there was a severe famine over all the land; yet Elijah was sent to none of them except to a widow at Zarephath in Sidon. There were also many lepers in Israel in the time of the prophet Elisha, and none of them was cleansed except Naaman the Syrian." When they heard this, all in the synagogue were filled with rage. They got up, drove him out of the town, and led him to the brow of the hill on which their town was built, so that they might hurl him off the cliff. But he passed through the midst of them and went on his way.

- The people here were jealous of their community of faith. Jesus was including all nationalities in the care and the saving love of God. They were jealous of their own relationship with God, and used it in many ordinary ways to keep others out.

- Jesus is the one of universal welcome, his heart open in prayer and life to all, no matter their creed, nation, gender, or age.

Tuesday 10th March
Matthew 18:21—22

Then Peter came and said to him, "Lord, if another member of the church sins against me, how often should I forgive? As many as seven times?" Jesus said to him, "Not seven times, but, I tell you, seventy-seven times."

- Jesus responds to Peter's generous benchmark of "seven times" by going even further—true forgiveness knows no limits at all.

- How do I express this in my own life; in my family, among my work colleagues, with my friends?

Wednesday 11th March
Matthew 5:17—19

Jesus said to his disciples, "Do not think that I have come to abolish the law or the prophets; I have come not to abolish but to fulfill. For truly I tell you, until heaven and earth pass away, not one letter, not one stroke of a letter, will pass from the law until all is accomplished. Therefore, whoever breaks one of the least of these commandments, and teaches others to do the same, will be called least in the kingdom of heaven; but whoever does them and teaches them will be called great in the kingdom of heaven."

- Jesus is no destroyer of people's devotions and faith. He does not abolish the faith practice of a people or a person. All the goodness of our religion and our faith is precious to him. His grace is given to each personally.

- Each of us prays differently, or with a variety of times, places, and moods. Prayer is entering into the mystery of God's love.

Thursday 12th March
Psalms 95:6—9

O come, let us worship and bow down. Let us kneel before the Lord, our Maker! For he is our God, and we are the people of his pasture, and the sheep of his hand. O that today you would listen to his voice! Do not harden your hearts, as at Meribah, as on the day at Massah in the wilderness, when your ancestors tested me, and put me to the proof, though they had seen my work.

- We all know the maxim, "Do not put off until tomorrow what you can do today." Instead, *carpe diem*—seize the moment, seize the day, do what needs to be done while you are still able, live like a hopeful person.

- Let me think about "today," and how I live. Am I putting off my response to Jesus, pushing it back until tomorrow?

Friday 13th March
Mark 12:28–34

One of the scribes came near and heard them disputing with one another, and seeing that he answered them well, he asked him, "Which commandment is the first of all?" Jesus answered, "The first is, 'Hear, O Israel: the Lord our God, the Lord is one; you shall love the Lord your God with all your heart, and with all your soul, and with all your mind, and with all your strength.' The second is this, 'You shall love your neighbor as yourself.' There is no other commandment greater than these."

Then the scribe said to him, "You are right, Teacher; you have truly said that 'he is one, and besides him there is no other'; and 'to love him with all the heart, and with all the understanding, and with all the strength,' and 'to love one's neighbor as oneself,'—this is much more important than all whole burnt offerings and sacrifices." When Jesus saw that he answered wisely, he said to him, "You are not far from the kingdom of God." After that no one dared to ask him any question.

- When we are committed to love, we are not far from the kingdom of God. It's like the open door to the kingdom.

- Our need for love sometimes brings us to darker places, so we need the help of God to bring us closer and closer to the sincerity and purity of love in God's kingdom.

Saturday 14th March
Luke 18:9–14

J esus also told this parable to some who
trusted in themselves that they were righteous
and regarded others with contempt: "Two men
went up to the Temple to pray, one a Pharisee
and the other a tax collector. The Pharisee,
standing by himself, was praying thus, 'God,
I thank you that I am not like other people:
thieves, rogues, adulterers, or even like this tax
collector. I fast twice a week; I give a tenth of all
my income.' But the tax collector, standing far
off, would not even look up to heaven, but was
beating his breast and saying, 'God, be merciful
to me, a sinner!' I tell you, this man went down
to his home justified rather than the other; for
all who exalt themselves will be humbled, but all
who humble themselves will be exalted."

- The contrast between the proud Pharisee and
  humble tax collector has entered so deeply into

our culture. To be a "Pharisee" in the time of Christ was a great honor. To be a "tax collector" was to live at the other end of the social spectrum. It would have been like being named a "convicted rapist" or "pedophile," or some other hated figure. We are sometimes persuaded to despise such people as the Pharisee despised the humble tax collector. Yet it is not for us to look down on anyone.

- How does the story hit me? I fear being an object of people's contempt. But Lord, if they knew me as you do, they might be right to feel contempt. I have no right to look down on those whose sins are paraded in the media. Be merciful to me.

March 15—21

Something to think and pray about each day this week:

Staying the Course

Long-term commitment—whether in marriage, religious life, or in any relationship—is harder these days because of change. The loved one changes, and we change ourselves with time, so our relationships change. We cannot live our whole lives at concert pitch. But when the tune changes, it need not be the end of the concert. It often is. In some countries, half the marriages end in divorce. What is there in us that can survive the changes of time, and the up-and-down of living relationships? As we look back at an anniversary or jubilee to celebrate twenty-five, forty, or even fifty years, we see our commitment is at once richer and more painful than when we started. Faithfulness is a bit of a mystery and a marvel; it has a value in itself. Faithful love builds up the one to whom we are faithful, expresses our hope in them. It is a grace, a gift: not so much what we do for God as what God does for us. It should make us feel humble—in spite of all our inadequacies, we stayed with it.

The Presence of God

I pause for a moment
and think of the love and the grace that God showers on me,
creating me in his image and likeness, making me his temple.

Freedom

Everything has the potential to draw forth from me a fuller love and life.
Yet my desires are often fixed, caught, on illusions of fulfillment.

I ask that God, through my freedom, may orchestrate
my desires in a vibrant loving melody rich in harmony.

Consciousness

In the presence of my loving Creator,
I look honestly at my feelings over the last day,
the highs, the lows, and the level ground.
Can I see where the Lord has been present?

The Word

God speaks to each one of us individually.
I need to listen to what he is saying to me.
(Please turn to your scripture on the following pages. Inspiration points are there should you need them. When you are ready, return here to continue.)

Conversation

What feelings are rising in me
as I pray and reflect on God's Word?

I imagine Jesus himself sitting or standing beside me,
and open my heart to him.

Conclusion

Glory be to the Father, and to the Son, and to the Holy Spirit,
As it was in the beginning, is now, and ever shall be,
World without end. Amen.

Sunday 15th March, Fourth Sunday of Lent
John 3:14—18

J esus said to Nicodemus, "And just as Moses lifted up the serpent in the wilderness, so must the Son of Man be lifted up, that whoever believes in him may have eternal life."

- Jesus is lifted up on the cross, and it is that same lifting that carries him into glory.

- As I look back on the bad times in my life, I can see how they brought me closer to you, Lord. No cross, no crown.

Monday 16th March
John 4:46b—54

N ow there was a royal official whose son lay ill in Capernaum. When he heard that Jesus had come from Judea to Galilee, he went and begged him to come down and heal his son, for he was at the point of death. Then Jesus said to him, "Unless you see signs and wonders you will not believe." The official said to him, "Sir, come down before my little boy dies." Jesus said to him, "Go; your son will live." The man believed the word that Jesus spoke to him and started on his way. As he was going down, his slaves met him and told him that his child was alive. So he asked them the hour when he began to recover, and they said to him, "Yesterday at one in the afternoon the fever left him." The father realized that this was the hour when Jesus had said to him, "Your son will live." So he himself believed, along with his whole household. Now this was the second sign that Jesus did after coming from Judea to Galilee.

- At first Jesus recoils; what he treasures is the company of those who want to know God for himself, not for what he can deliver. The father returns as a believer, and Jesus welcomes him.

- Lord, forgive me for the times I have turned to you in a crisis, begging a favor. When the crisis passes, I go back to living as though you do not exist. I want to find time for you.

Tuesday 17th March,
St. Patrick
Matthew 13:31—33

Jesus put before them another parable: "The kingdom of heaven is like a mustard seed that someone took and sowed in his field; it is the smallest of all the seeds, but when it has grown it is the greatest of shrubs and becomes a tree, so that the birds of the air come and make nests in its branches." He told them another parable: "The kingdom of heaven is like yeast that a woman took and mixed in with three measures of flour until all of it was leavened."

• May the Strength of God guide us. May the Power of God preserve us. May the Wisdom of God instruct us. May the Hand of God protect us. May the Way of God direct us. May the

Shield of God defend us. May the Angels of God guard us against the snares of the evil one.

- May Christ be with us! May Christ be before us! May Christ be in us! May Christ be in us, Christ be over all! May Thy Grace, Lord, Always be ours, This day, O Lord, and forevermore. Amen.

Wednesday 18th March
Psalm 144 (145):8—9, 13—14

The Lord is gracious and merciful, slow to anger and abounding in steadfast love. The Lord is good to all, and his compassion is over all that he has made. Your kingdom is an everlasting kingdom, and your dominion endures throughout all generations. The Lord is faithful in all his words, and gracious in all his deeds. The Lord upholds all who are falling, and raises up all who are bowed down.

- The psalmists put their trust in the loving God of Israel, their king, their rock, their refuge, their shepherd. This is not a god of wrath, but the God of compassion, love, and forgiveness.

- In whom do I trust? Is it in a loving, forgiving God?

Thursday 19th March,
St. Joseph
Matthew 1:18—25

Now the birth of Jesus the Messiah took place in this way. When his mother Mary had been engaged to Joseph, but before they lived together, she was found to be with child from the Holy Spirit. Her husband Joseph, being a righteous man and unwilling to expose her to public disgrace, planned to dismiss her quietly. But just when he had resolved to do this, an angel of the Lord appeared to him in a dream and said, "Joseph, son of David, do not be afraid to take Mary as your wife, for the child conceived in her is from the Holy Spirit. She will bear a son, and you are to name him Jesus, for he will save his people from their sins." All this took place to fulfill what had been spoken by the Lord through the prophet: "Look, the virgin shall conceive and bear a son, and they shall name him Emmanuel," which means, "God is with us." When Joseph awoke from sleep, he did as the angel of the Lord commanded him; he took her as his wife, but had no marital relations with her until she had borne a son; and he named him Jesus.

- Joseph is the patron of carers—in love and work he cared for his dearest ones. He was a man of faith who learned from the angels of God what was needed of him, and did the same. Jesus did as he did, and found some of the best qualities in his life from the people he grew up with, Joseph and Mary.

- Can I pray today for those who cared for me as I grew into faith and love?

Friday 20th March
John 7:25–30

Now some of the people of Jerusalem were saying, "Is not this the man whom they are trying to kill? And here he is, speaking openly, but they say nothing to him! Can it be that the authorities really know that this is the Messiah? Yet we know where this man is from; but when the Messiah comes, no one will know where he is from." Then Jesus cried out as he was teaching in the temple, "You know me, and you know where I am from. I have not come on my own. But the one who sent me is true, and you do not know him. I know him, because I am from him, and he sent me." Then they tried to arrest him, but no one laid hands on him, because his hour had not yet come.

- Jesus lived all his public life under the danger of death. He lived in that awareness of mortal danger.

- But he seems to be the one in control, even though powers of evil and death surround him. He would choose his hour.

Saturday 21st March
John 7:40—47

When they heard these words, some in the crowd said, "This is really the prophet." Others said, "This is the Messiah." But some asked, "Surely the Messiah does not come from Galilee, does he? Has not the scripture said that the Messiah is descended from David and comes from Bethlehem, the village where David lived?" So there was a division in the crowd because of him. Some of them wanted to arrest him, but no one laid hands on him. Then the temple police went back to the chief priests and Pharisees, who asked them, "Why did you not arrest him?" The police answered, "Never has anyone spoken like this!" Then the Pharisees replied, "Surely you have not been deceived too, have you?"

- Many were amazed at the power of the words of Jesus. They whispered to each other that nobody else spoke like him. His authority both influenced them and challenged them. Many tried to put him down for where he came from, but their disbelief didn't influence everyone else. He was a sign of contradiction.

March 22—28

Something to think and pray about each day this week:

Slowing Down

These weeks leading to Good Friday can have a special poignancy as we grow older, a regret that Jesus never lived to middle or old age, but died when he was thirty-three, at the height of his powers. We do not know from the Gospels how he would have coped with sickness, accidents, the loss of friends, failure in work, the slowing of the mind, the lapses of memory, the aching limbs, the sense that life has passed its peak. All these things happened to him suddenly, in twenty-four hours, from Thursday evening to Friday afternoon. To us they happen slowly, with more time for us to accept them well or badly.

They are, more than any individual tragedy, our crucifixion, our share in Jesus' fate.

The Presence of God

I reflect for a moment on God's presence around me and in me.
Creator of the universe, the sun and the moon, the earth,
every molecule, every atom, everything that is:
God is in every beat of my heart. God is with me now.

Freedom

A thick and shapeless tree-trunk would never believe
that it could become a statue, admired as a miracle of sculpture,
and would never submit itself to the chisel of the sculptor,
who sees by her genius what she can make of it (St. Ignatius).

I ask for the grace to let myself be shaped by
my loving Creator.

Consciousness

Knowing that God loves me unconditionally,
I look honestly over the last day, its events and
my feelings.
Do I have something to be grateful for? Then I
give thanks.
Is there something I am sorry for? Then I ask
forgiveness.

The Word

I read the Word of God slowly, a few times
over, and I listen to what God is saying to me.
(Please turn to your scripture on the following
pages. Inspiration points are there should you
need them. When you are ready, return here to
continue.)

Conversation

What is stirring in me as I pray?

Am I consoled, troubled, left cold?
I imagine Jesus himself standing or sitting at my side,
and share my feelings with him.

Conclusion
Glory be to the Father, and to the Son, and to the Holy Spirit,
As it was in the beginning, is now, and ever shall be,
World without end. Amen.

Sunday 22nd March,
Fifth Sunday of Lent
John 12:20—24

N ow among those who went up to worship at the festival were some Greeks. They came to Philip, who was from Bethsaida in Galilee, and said to him, "Sir, we wish to see Jesus." Philip went and told Andrew; then Andrew and Philip went and told Jesus. Jesus answered them, "The hour has come for the Son of Man to be glorified. Very truly, I tell you, unless a grain of wheat falls into the earth and dies, it remains just a single grain; but if it dies, it bears much fruit."

- What the Greeks asked of Philip is what Christians have been seeking in the Gospels and in pilgrimages for two thousand years: "We wish to see Jesus." When they found him, they heard those pregnant words: A grain of wheat has to die before it bears fruit.

- Only in Jesus have we a person and a philosophy that makes sense of suffering and death, and that sees the life beyond them.

Monday 23rd March
Daniel 13:55–56, 60–62

Daniel said, "Indeed! Your lie recoils on you own head: the angel of God has already received from him your sentence and will cut you in half." He dismissed the man, ordered the other to be brought and said to him, "Son of Canaan, not of Judah, beauty has seduced you, lust has led your heart astray!" ... Then the whole assembly shouted, blessing God, the Saviour of those who trust in him. And they turned on the two elders whom Daniel had convicted of false evidence out of their own mouths. As the Law of Moses prescribes, they were given the same punishment as they had schemed to inflict on their neighbour. They were put to death. And thus, that day, an innocent life was saved.

- These are not happy characters. Dissipation and addiction are forms of imprisonment in which the chains are inside you, not outside, so the pain is greater. The German ("God is dead") philosopher Nietzsche stated the downside of lust: "The mother of dissipation is not joy, but joylessness." Thomas Aquinas put it more positively: "A joyful heart is a sure sign of temperance and self-control." Do I show that sign?

Tuesday 24th March
John 8:21–30

Again Jesus said to them, "I am going away, and you will search for me, but you will die in your sin. Where I am going, you cannot come." Then the Jews said, "Is he going to kill himself? Is that what he means by saying, 'Where I am going, you cannot come'?" He said to them, "You are from below, I am from above; you are of this world, I am not of this world. I told you that you would die in your sins, for you will die in your sins unless you believe that I am he." They said to him, "Who are you?" Jesus said to them, "Why do I speak to you at all? I have much to say about you and much to condemn; but the one who sent me is true, and I declare to the world what I have heard from him." They did not understand that he was speaking to them about the Father. So Jesus said to them, "When you have lifted up the Son of Man, then you will realize that I am he, and that I do nothing on my own, but I speak these things as the Father instructed me. And the one who sent me is with me; he has not left me alone, for I always do what is pleasing to him." As he was saying these things, many believed in him.

- Jesus had a sense in his life that he was not left alone. Even on the cross he did not seem alone, crying out, "My God, my God, why have you forsaken me?"

- In Jesus we are all loved by the Father and in our lives—even in the most extreme moments—are never left alone.

Wednesday 25th March
The Annunciation
Luke 1:26–33

In the sixth month the angel Gabriel was sent by God to a town in Galilee called Nazareth, to a virgin whose name was Mary. And he came to her and said, "Greetings, favored one! The Lord is with you." But she was much perplexed by his words and pondered what sort of greeting this might be. The angel said to her, "Do not be afraid, Mary, for you have found favour with God. And now, you will conceive in your womb and bear a son, and you will name him Jesus. He will be great, and will be called the Son of the Most High, and the Lord God will give to him the throne of his ancestor David. He will reign over the house of Jacob forever, and of his kingdom there will be no end."

- As with Mary, God announces to each of us that we are called to the work of the Son of God. Our vocation in life is first that we have found favour with God, and God is with us. Then we are asked to allow the life of God to reach deeply into our lives so that the divine life and love reaches others through each of us.

- Each of us can be a part of the plan of God to love and save the world.

Thursday 26th March
John 8:54—59

Jesus said to the Jews, "If I glorify myself, my glory is nothing. It is my Father who glorifies me, he of whom you say, 'He is our God,' though you do not know him. But I know him; if I were to say that I do not know him, I would be a liar like you. But I do know him and I keep his word. Your ancestor Abraham rejoiced that he would see my day; he saw it and was glad." Then the Jews said to him, "You are not yet fifty years old, and have you seen Abraham?" Jesus said to them, "Very truly, I tell you, before Abraham was, I am." So they picked up stones to throw at him, but Jesus hid himself and went out of the temple.

- The Word of God has a powerful effect and leads us to life that is everlasting. The Word of God begins in heaven, lives on earth for a short time, and returns to heaven, promising us the same.

- The mystery of these weeks of the passion and death of Jesus links heaven and earth in a wide and wonderful bond of love.

Friday 27th March
John 10:31—38

The Jews took up stones again to stone him. Jesus replied, "I have shown you many good works from the Father. For which of these are you going to stone me?" The Jews answered,

"It is not for a good work that we are going to stone you, but for blasphemy, because you, though only a human being, are making yourself God." Jesus answered, "Is it not written in your law, 'I said, you are gods'? If those to whom the word of God came were called 'gods'—and the scripture cannot be annulled—can you say that the one whom the Father has sanctified and sent into the world is blaspheming because I said, 'I am God's Son'? If I am not doing the works of my Father, then do not believe me. But if I do them, even though you do not believe me, believe the works, so that you may know and understand that the Father is in me and I am in the Father."

- The works of healing, teaching, and forgiveness were among other works of Jesus done in the name of God. All of Jesus leads us to his divine origin, the Son and Word of God. Something more than human seemed to touch others through him, as some believed and many did not.

- May I be led to an ever deeper faith in the divine Son of God.

Saturday 28th March
John 11:47—52

So the chief priests and the Pharisees called a meeting of the council, and said, "What are we to do? This man is performing many signs. If we let him go on like this, everyone will believe in him, and the Romans will come and destroy both our holy place and our nation." But one of them, Caiaphas, who was high priest that year, said to them, "You know nothing at all! You do not understand that it is better for you to have one man die for the people than to have the whole nation destroyed." He did not say this on his own, but being high priest that year he prophesied that Jesus was about to die for the nation, and not for the nation only, but to gather into one the dispersed children of God.

- Numerous men and women have been the one victim for many.

- In the eyes of the religious leaders of his time, Jesus signed his death warrant the day he said to a paralyzed man, "Your sins are forgiven," thus making claim to be God. We simply accompany him these days as he approaches death and torture.

- We remember people in our world today who still suffer torture.

March 29 — April 4

Something to think and pray about each day this week:

The Triumph of Suffering

Holy Week, as it is called, marked the steepest learning curve in the lives of Jesus' disciples, and we might gear our prayer to the events and lessons of each day. It seemed to start well, with the Hosannas of Palm Sunday. Jesus, mounted on a donkey, entered Jerusalem in triumph (Luke 19:28). But he had no illusions. Approaching the city he wept over it, "If you had only understood the message of peace!" As we watch the Passion unfold, we can appreciate the verdict of Saint Peter Claver, who spent his life in the holds of slave-ships, ministering to African victims condemned to hopeless suffering: "The only book people should read is the Passion."

Or St. Thérèse of Lisieux, in the anguish of her last illness: "What does it mean to have written beautiful words about suffering. Nothing! Nothing! One must experience it to know what such effusions are worth." In prayer this week we need to live with the taste of pain and triumphant evil.

The Presence of God

In the silence of my innermost being,
in the fragments of my yearned-for wholeness,
can I hear the whispers of God's presence?
Can I remember when I felt God's nearness?
When we walked together and I let myself be
embraced by God's love.

Freedom

There are very few people
who realize what God would make of them
if they abandoned themselves into his hands,

and let themselves be formed by his grace (St. Ignatius).

I ask for the grace to trust myself totally to God's love.

Consciousness

How do I find myself today?

Where am I with God? With others?

Do I have something to be grateful for? Then I give thanks.

Is there something I am sorry for? Then I ask forgiveness.

The Word

I take my time to read the Word of God, slowly, a few times, allowing myself to dwell on anything that strikes me. (Please turn to your scripture on the following pages. Inspiration points are there should you need them. When you are ready, return here to continue.)

Conversation

Do I notice myself reacting as I pray with the
Word of God?
Do I feel challenged, comforted, angry?
Imagining Jesus sitting or standing by me,
I speak out my feelings, as one trusted friend
to another.

Conclusion

Glory be to the Father, and to the Son, and to
the Holy Spirit,
As it was in the beginning, is now, and ever
shall be,
World without end. Amen.

Sunday 29th March,
Palm Sunday of the Lord's Passion
Philippians 2:6–11

Let the same mind be in you that was in Christ Jesus, who, though he was in the form of God, did not regard equality with God as something to be exploited, but emptied himself, taking the form of a slave, being born in human likeness. And being found in human form, he humbled himself and became obedient to the point of death—even death on a cross. Therefore God also highly exalted him and gave him the name that is above every name, so that at the name of Jesus every knee should bend, in heaven and on earth and under the earth, and every tongue should confess that Jesus Christ is Lord, to the glory of God the Father.

• On this Sunday of the Passion, we read St. Paul's Christ-hymn, which offers a dense theology of the Incarnation. Jesus emptied himself and accepted the loss of everything—family, power, the love and respect of his own people, and finally his own life.

• Lord, you ask me to have the same mind as you had. I can accept the emptying out of my attachments because you have shown me the way.

Monday 30th March
John 12:1—6

Six days before the Passover Jesus came to Bethany, the home of Lazarus, whom he had raised from the dead. There they gave a dinner for him. Martha served, and Lazarus was one of those at the table with him. Mary took a pound of costly perfume made of pure nard, anointed Jesus' feet, and wiped them with her hair. The house was filled with the fragrance of the perfume. But Judas Iscariot, one of his disciples (the one who was about to betray him), said, "Why was this perfume not sold for three hundred denarii and the money given to the poor?" (He said this not because he cared about the poor, but because he was a thief; he kept the common purse and used to steal what was put into it.)

- The anointing of Jesus' feet may represent the generosity of Mary: she gave without holding back, without being constrained by the logic of thoughts like those of Judas.

- Lord, help me to pray with generosity, to give my time without mean-spirited thoughts about what else I might be doing.

Tuesday 31st March
John 13:31—33, 36—38

When Judas had gone out, Jesus said, "Now the Son of Man has been glorified, and God has been glorified in him. If God has been glorified in him, God will also glorify him in himself and will glorify him at once. Little children, I am with you only a little longer. You will look for me; and as I said to the

Jews so now I say to you, 'Where I am going, you cannot come.'" Simon Peter said to him, "Lord, where are you going?" Jesus answered, "Where I am going, you cannot follow me now; but you will follow afterwards." Peter said to him, "Lord, why can I not follow you now? I will lay down my life for you." Jesus answered, "Will you lay down your life for me? Very truly, I tell you, before the cock crows, you will have denied me three times."

- Peter hit deep points of his life here. His sureness in following Jesus was challenged by Jesus himself. He would later find himself weak and failing in this following.

- But this would not be the last word; even when Peter said later that he didn't know Jesus, there would be time for taking it back and speaking it with his life.

- We oscillate in our following of the Lord. These days let us know in the certainty of Jesus' love that there is always another day, another chance, another joy in our following of Jesus.

Wednesday 1st April
Matthew 26:14–16, 20–25

Then one of the twelve, who was called Judas Iscariot, went to the chief priests and said, "What will you give me if I betray him to you?" They paid him thirty pieces of silver. And from that moment he began to look for an opportunity to betray him. When it was evening, Jesus took his place with the twelve; and while they were eating, he said, "Truly I tell you, one of you will betray me." And they became greatly distressed and began to say to him one after another, "Surely not I, Lord?" He answered, "The one who has dipped his hand into the bowl with me will betray me. The Son of Man goes as it is written of him, but woe to that one by whom the Son of Man is betrayed! It would have been better for that one not to have been born."

Judas, who betrayed him, said, "Surely not I, Rabbi?" He replied, "You have said so."

- "Thirty pieces of silver" is a phrase that retains its currency today, describing the worst type of treachery. Jesus suffered this much in his passion.

- The man of suffering is the God who still suffers the pain, injustices, greed, and betrayal of his people today. God is not impervious to our suffering.

- Our prayer can be simply to be with him in his suffering, trying to feel as he felt, to think as he thought.

Thursday 2nd April, Holy Thursday
John 13:2–15

During supper Jesus, knowing that the Father had given all things into his hands and that he had come from God and was going to God, got up from the table, took off his outer robe, and tied a towel around himself. Then he poured water into a basin and began to wash the disciples' feet and to wipe them with the towel that was tied around him. He came to Simon Peter, who said to him, "Lord, are you going to wash my feet?" Jesus answered, "You do not know now what I am doing, but later you will understand." Peter said to him, "You will never wash my feet." Jesus answered, "Unless I wash you, you have no share with me." Simon Peter said to him, "Lord, not my feet only but also my hands and my head!" Jesus said to him, "One who has bathed does not need to wash, except for the feet, but is entirely clean. And you are clean, though not all of you." For he knew who was to betray him; for this reason he said, "Not all of you are clean." After Jesus had washed their feet, had put on his robe, and had returned to the table, he said to them, "Do you know what I have done to you? You call me Teacher and Lord—and you are right, for that is what I am. So if I, your Lord and Teacher, have washed your feet, you also ought to wash one another's feet. For I have set you an example, that you also should do as I have done to you."

- There's much in the gospel story or words of Jesus that we can't immediately understand. He says little about the meaning of the washing of the feet, except that it's about service, and then just that we should do it too.

- By doing something in the example or name of Jesus, we often find its meaning. Or by just listening to his word, it begins to make sense. This is heart-knowledge and prayer-knowledge.

Friday 3rd April, Good Friday
John 19:25—30

Meanwhile, standing near the cross of Jesus were his mother and his mother's sister, Mary the wife of Clopas, and Mary Magdalene. When Jesus saw his mother and the disciple whom he loved standing beside her, he said to his mother, "Woman, here is your son." Then he said to the disciple, "Here is your mother." And from that hour the disciple took her into his own home. After this, when Jesus knew that all was now finished, he said (in order to fulfill the scripture), "I am thirsty." A jar full of sour wine was standing there. So they put a sponge full of the wine on a branch of hyssop and held it to his mouth. When Jesus had received the wine, he said, "It is finished." Then he bowed his head and gave up his spirit.

- All of us will one day give up our spirit. All of us will one day say, either with words, breath, or gesture, that it is finished. It will not be like Jesus on a cross, but it may be in pain or in loneliness or in fear.

- We can offer our death to God; we can do so with Mary—"Holy Mary, mother of God, pray for us, sinners; now and at the hour of our death."

Saturday 4th April,
Holy Saturday
Matthew 27:57—66

When it was evening, there came a rich man from Arimathea, named Joseph, who was also a disciple of Jesus. He went to Pilate and asked for the body of Jesus; then Pilate ordered it to be given to him. So Joseph took the body and wrapped it in a clean linen cloth and laid it in his own new tomb, which he had hewn in the rock. He then rolled a great stone to the door of the tomb and went away. Mary Magdalene and the other Mary were there, sitting opposite the tomb. The next day, that is, after the day of Preparation, the chief priests and the Pharisees gathered before Pilate and said, "Sir, we remember what that impostor said while he was still alive, 'After three days I will rise again.' Therefore command that the tomb be made secure until the third day; otherwise his disciples may go and steal him away, and tell the people, 'He has been raised from the dead,' and the last deception would be worse than the first." Pilate said to them, "You have a guard of soldiers; go, make it as secure as you can." So they went with the guard and made the tomb secure by sealing the stone.

- The Saturday of Holy Week can be an empty day as we wait and wait for the evening of resurrection. Like the ones who had placed Jesus kindly in their tomb, we wait with him for something new. With Jesus there is always the hint of something new, and even at the tomb they were afraid he might rise.

- We pray in hope this day—the wood of the cross had within it the sap of hope. It may look like a dead tree, but it is alive with expectation.

April 5

Something to think and pray about today:

The Body of Life

On the first Easter morning, the apostles and the holy women did not see a ghost of Jesus. They saw him in the flesh, but in a different flesh, as the oak tree is different from the acorn that was its origin. We touch on the mystery of a body, not just Jesus' body but our own, which will express us at our best, will not blunt our spirit with weariness and rebellion, but express it with ease and joy. The Lord knows my name and my body. He sees my lived-in face, shaped by my history, showing the lines of love, indulgence, suffering, humor, gentleness. As the proverb says, "The face you have at forty is the face that you deserve." Teach me to love my face and body, my temple of the Holy Spirit. It will grow old and die with me, but that is not the end.

This is a mystery beyond our imagination, but it is the centre of our faith. As we grow older, nothing in our faith makes more sense than the Passion and the Resurrection, the certainty that our bodies, like Jesus', must suffer and die, and the certainty that we, in our bodies, have a life beyond death. When we wish one another a happy Easter, it is not just three days in an armchair, but also deep joy in the knowledge that the best part of us will cheat the grave. Our weary bones, heavy flesh, addled brains already hold the seeds of that resurrection. We are none of us mortal.

The Presence of God

God is with me, but more,
God is within me, giving me existence.
Let me dwell for a moment on God's life-giving presence

in my body, my mind, my heart,
and in the whole of my life.

Freedom

Many countries are at this moment suffering
the agonies of war.
I bow my head in thanksgiving for my
freedom.
I pray for all prisoners and captives.

Consciousness

I remind myself that I am in the presence of
the Lord.
I will take refuge in His loving heart.
He is my strength in times of weakness.
He is my comforter in times of sorrow.

The Word

I read the Word of God slowly, a few times
over, and I listen to what God is saying to me.
(Please turn to your scripture on the following
pages. Inspiration points are there should you

need them. When you are ready, return here to continue.)

Conversation

How has God's Word moved me? Has it left me cold?

Has it consoled me or moved me to act in a new way?

I imagine Jesus standing or sitting beside me, I turn and share my feelings with him.

Conclusion

Glory be to the Father, and to the Son, and to the Holy Spirit,

As it was in the beginning, is now, and ever shall be,

World without end. Amen.

Sunday 5th April,
Easter Sunday
John 20:1—9

Early on the first day of the week, while it was still dark, Mary Magdalene came to the tomb and saw that the stone had been removed from the tomb. So she ran and went to Simon Peter and the other disciple, the one whom Jesus loved, and said to them, "They have taken the Lord out of the tomb, and we do not know where they have laid him." Then Peter and the other disciple set out and went toward the tomb. The two were running together, but the other disciple outran Peter and reached the tomb first. He bent down to look in and saw the linen wrappings lying there, but he did not go in. Then Simon Peter came, following him, and went into the tomb. He saw the linen wrappings lying there, and the cloth that had been on Jesus' head, not lying with the linen wrappings but rolled up in a place by itself. Then the other disciple, who reached the tomb first, also went in, and he saw and believed; for as yet they did not understand the scripture, that he must rise from the dead.

- Whenever we share compassion, justice, reconciliation, faith, and encourage each other to be people of hope, we are people of the resurrection and ministers of the resurrection.

- Jesus is raised from death each time we live his way of life. We do this in our various ways by showing care and concern for the lives and troubles of others.

- Lord, teach me to be a minister of the resurrection.

Traditional Ignatian Prayers to Pray throughout the Day

Morning Prayer

God our Father, I offer you today
all that I think and do and say.
I offer it with what was done
on earth by Jesus Christ, your Son.
Amen.

Morning Offering

My God, I offer you my prayers,
my works, my joys, and my sufferings of this day
in union with the holy sacrifice of the Mass throughout the world.

I offer them for all the intentions of your Son's Sacred Heart,
for the salvation of souls, reparation for sin,

and the reunion of Christians.
Amen.

Evening Prayer

God, our Father, this day is done.
We ask you and Jesus Christ, your Son,
that with the Spirit, our most welcome guest,
you guard our sleep and bless our rest.
Amen.

The *Suscipe*

Take, Lord, and receive all my liberty,
my memory, my understanding,
and my entire will,
All I have and call my own.

You have given all to me.
To you, Lord, I return it.

Everything is yours. Do with it what you will.
Give me only your love and your grace,
that is enough for me.

Prayer for Generosity

Eternal Word, only begotten Son of God,

Teach me true generosity.

Teach me to serve you as you deserve.

To give without counting the cost,

To fight heedless of wounds,

To labor without seeking rest,

To sacrifice myself without thought of any
reward

Save the knowledge that I have done your will.

Amen.

Anima Christi

Soul of Christ, sanctify me.

Body of Christ, save me.

Blood of Christ, inebriate me.

Water from the side of Christ, wash me.

Passion of Christ, strengthen me.

O Good Jesus, hear me.

Within your wounds hide me.

April 2015

Permit me not to be separated from you.

From the wicked foe, defend me.

At the hour of my death, call me and bid me

come to you

That with your saints I may praise you

For ever and ever. Amen.

Founded in 1865, Ave Maria Press,
a ministry of the Congregation of
Holy Cross, is a Catholic publishing
company that serves the spiritual and
formative needs of the Church and its
schools, institutions, and ministers;
Christian individuals and families; and
others seeking spiritual nourishment.

For a complete listing of titles from

Ave Maria Press

Sorin Books

Forest of Peace

Christian Classics

visit www.avemariapress.com

ave maria press® / Notre Dame, IN 46556
A Ministry of the United States Province of Holy Cross

The Irish Jesuits are engaged in a wide range of ministries both at home and throughout the world. They serve as teachers, caregivers for homeless youth, parish priests, academics, artists, and administrators. Their website, *Sacred Space*, attracts more than six million visits annually and is produced in some twenty languages.